DIVIDE
AND
RULE

DIVIDE AND RULE

WALID BITAR

COACH HOUSE BOOKS
TORONTO

first edition

 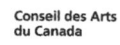 

Published with the generous assistance of the Canada Council for the Arts and the Ontario Arts Council. Coach House Books also acknowledges the support of the Government of Canada through the Canada Book Fund and the Government of Ontario through the Ontario Book Publishing Tax Credit.

LIBRARY AND ARCHIVES CANADA CATALOGUING IN PUBLICATION

Bitar, Walid, 1961-
   Divide and rule / Walid Bitar.

Poems.
ISBN 978-1-55245-254-7

   I. Title.

PS8553.I87755D58 2012   C811'.54   C2012-900236-4

Divide and Rule is available as an ebook: ISBN 978 1 77056 305 6.

Visit www.chbooks.com/digital to claim your free digital download of this book. Use the code D151R0B83W when prompted. Customers may be required to demonstrate proof of purchase. (Coach House reserves the right to terminate the free digital download offer at any time.)

THE POEMS

MISSION CREEP

Big, small and medium-sized,
fish whose schools I didn't dynamite
the first blockade or two, mission creep
setting in now – flames children burst into,

we elders sit around telling fairytales,
sick of you as you are of us,
patients concealing serious symptoms.
The sun behind you, you could eclipse,

if you were the moon. Words often fail
at the last minute that arrives too early.
Seems you're currently at a loss for them;
here they are. Listen how? Carefully,

hunger-striker. Sing for my supper,
and you prove the whatchamacallit
would never land on your broad shoulders,
as if it were a parakeet – bolt of lightning,

more like, though that isn't it either.
I'm at a standstill, not up to scratch,
dependent as pawns are on chessboards –
rooks, kings, queens, the grandmaster's

spring offensive supposedly launched
because the white Christmases wouldn't stop.
If the obvious isn't made obvious,
there's no telling what it may become.

THE GOOD REASON

The stratagems of the enemy,
subject of pre-war conversation,
wiped smiles off his and our faces
when reality became unspeakable.

I loved him once – may he rest assured
in a crypt I spent the morning sealing.
I awoke feeling misunderstood,
therefore decided I'd clear my throat,

carve in stone maxims inchoate
when I was in a better position
to mutter something, mean nothing by it.
Now I'm forced to act after I speak

in our circle of mandarins,
some intimating they need a bit extra
to distinguish them from their closest friends
on whom they turn, barbarism feigned.

How did we lose the shared sense of humour
claimed later by each as his own?
There are various versions of events,
the solution conflating them all

before they multiply, the gossip
in both my ears, and out both others.
The good reason: I hired a double
the research shows helps a man grow,

grasping though I am for ideals
formerly held at a lesser distance.
Almost as easy wrestling free
as raising arms high in surrender,

regaling audiences, their feet of clay
not any archetypal model's,
so I must sculpt them. Rather painful –
mission accomplished with an iron fist.

THE HUNDRED-METRE HURDLES

Hypnotize me, an emancipated
slave compromised by tacit acceptance
of the status quo – may I flow faster
than flash-flood water down the drains

into the sea. Doesn't look like rain,
background of your still life you're angry
I sell as a paint-by-numbers set,
or a thousand-piece jigsaw puzzle.

Didn't stick my leg out – you tripped
single-handedly after a few,
a very few, too many. Self-hatred's
career-threatening. There's much I owe

you for diverting unbearable pressure.
Wait until you regain consciousness
from a beating I'll resume administering
and, in the meantime, lick my own wounds,

blisters I prick after state-sponsored walking –
transliterated, the names of athletes
caught clearing hurdles, or knocking them over.
Wouldn't underestimate this rabble

if I were their coach. I'm of their number,
must compete in our teeming slum.
Trash-talking beggars I grant pardons.
Something I wouldn't call a conscience

serves me, like Rottweiler or seneschal.
Since I can't afford either, the sound
of my thinking out loud suffices.
Laugh at it – it becomes the laughter.

SOUND BARRIER

Publically, you claim you're an ocean
I am surviving in as marine life,
without provoking a rival's claque,
its main body on a beach frying,

predictable before the sun descends
to an underworld we're above at war.
I'd rather fight the living. The dead
have had too much time to mull things over,

argue their questions precede statements
I issue, turning my words into answers,
though I speak first – there's no respect
for simple chronology from the bastards,

their testes crated, and ours in states
required by the counter-revolution,
our ex-employer preaching from the choir,
singing never his primary strength,

glorious, though, compared to splashes
through swamps whose sprites mistook us for ephemera
they'd carelessly created with snaps
of fingers they later realized we'd fractured,

divine punishment a lower sound barrier,
our speech's value incalculable
as oxygen's, because regular users
are sometimes the rich, sometimes the poor,

these beasts of burden driving me wild
till I'm so comfortable in my skin
I fall back on memories I shouldn't trust,
and don't expect they'll break my fall.

DIGGING A HOLE

Heavily censored, how tunnellers live:
as we please, around here, an elite –
in the majority, persons of interest
cultivating for rices and beans.

I jump beautifully out of the way
before a backlash our lower classes
consider a right: holding the noble man's
feet to a fire he carelessly sets.

Dance, my eldest shall study abroad.
Rather than institutions of higher
learning, I chose water muddied
by my dirty shoes, peered into depths

and started digging a hole, first step
toward destabilizing the planet,
its orbit difficult to disturb,
its hot core solid, or I'd fan the flames.

CONTRACTORS

This phony warrior's armed to the teeth,
our barks and his bites all but synchronized,
the son of a bitch – I mean, of a state
that doesn't love him, and he doesn't love.

Dash upstairs – praise to the skies
what might fall on us if it isn't in them,
yours no future money couldn't buy,
or, failing that, at least destroy.

Do me this favour and, in exchange,
I'll mask ingratitude; a disguise
overwhelms the plain truths any day.
It looks like somebody, and so do I,

most at home under another's name –
not just an alias – in another's thoughts,
yours for example. They irritate me
a little less than if I had had them.

AN IMMIGRANT

They're good judges, or they wouldn't have risen
slowly so far. I wasn't their pilot;
I was presiding. Did they obey orders?
Didn't give any. Clinging to power,

I paid for services, expected miracles
and am waiting around with the patience
of a besieger, thus can't surrender.
I'll see the light, allow that it's faint,

suppress a narrow range of emotions
you assumed extinct till informed exotic
jungles they're from survive in a foreign,
partially peeled banana republic

whose dictator disgusts me personally,
though he and I are both larger than life,
and terrified of death. What does that leave?
I am in a position to compromise,

will spare you grammar in your harsh sentences,
if you solve this puzzle: a mulatto
won't accept our lovable greenbacks
as proper payment for his petroleum,

demands from us illegal rain checks,
his drought-stricken godforsaken country
mine for crying out loud. I was born there.
Should I, like any immigrant, save my skin?

If you concentrate, pleasure and pain
rise to the levels of happiness
and suffering. I once shovelled manure by day –
by night, this sight for sore eyes: bullshit,

the pure kind, inhuman, not animal,
I'd find a better way to describe,
if that were in my interest. It isn't.
You'll never tame me. I was never wild.

THE LOW VOLUMES

A born acrobat's, your gospel – you leap
whenever caught losing an argument,
frozen in headlights beside the deer,
smash through glass and you're in the driver's seat,

suddenly conscious the mysteries of death
are only experienced by survivors.
Some believe in a live-and-let-live
manifesto, our arch-enemies;

they refuse a fight – rather difficult
convincing them there's a war in progress.
How many of their number must we kill
before they evolve into semblances of us,

throw a few punches at least, right wrongs?
Things look up because of the certainty
with which – look, no hands – my views hold
water as if it were already ice,

my range so wide framing it's a problem:
proud one moment, and the next vain,
I compromise, pass for vainglorious,
though I'm honest enough to keep changing

the low volumes of my inner voices,
inaudible unless I shut my trap,
turn a blind eye to the justice system,
since it poked the eye out in the first place.

EXACT CHANGE

I wonder how you'll react tomorrow
when you're shaken well, and remember
me in your dreams, interpreting for you
as you slept – will you tender thanks?

Anything can happen, yet our days
pass in such a predictable manner
the organized take an interest in –
there is the difference between us and them.

I've seen my share of the whole earth on spec –
I want the sum of parts it doesn't have.
A holy man learns, deflects attention
away from himself and onto a rosary.

A lesser trickster, I pen the odd proverb,
warn my victims, this chivalrous streak
among the improbable side effects
when I split my personality,

an experiment most could do without,
but I have no choice, must continue using
power I, of all people, inherited,
and by which I feel persecuted,

prizing, far more than the collective
weight of an army busting my scales,
the ability of a single detective
I hire to hand me the exact change.

THE WISH

In your last fight to the death, you discovered
it was for death you were willing to die,
a more logical cause than the others,
because you'd grown very tired of life,

free will exercised. You decided
on a necessary course of action,
planted your flag in torrential rain,
then slipped through cracks in drying mud.

Until this storm, artificially lit,
the studios behind your every move,
you did no wrong that wasn't set right
by the time you rose in the morning,

my punches thrown years before they landed.
While waiting, I put food on the table
in minimum-wage cameos counting raindrops
instead of clouds, which are much easier,

though I forgive everything today.
Thanks for the memories worth less than toys,
and more than candles blown out, the wish
my big secret. I'm birthday boy,

overexcited, forgetting criteria
checked off before balance is regained,
too far down a road back to chaos
out of which my touch of class was created,

as were your silences on the rack,
until the tuning fork vibrated.
Sabbaths, our modest powers-that-be
pass the hat for a little night music.

SCORCHED EARTH POLICY

I can't beat your ignorance senseless –
it's an idea, unaware it's for real,
like wisdom actually. Grant me this much:
I never found the golden mean tempting,

my dates with destiny, marriage arranged,
years bragging about rights to bear arms
ending in some kind of engagement with
loggers turning roots into a living –

beneath the dignity of our autochtonous
factotums a devious Druid trained
to tread water they couldn't hop on.
Their whistle-stop we napalmed boomed,

our main chance jumped at, ground hit running.
You'll never see the forest, for the trees
your points of view excluded don't exist now,
on account of the scorched earth policy.

GRAVE ROBBERS

It was during my penultimate escape
attempt I determined I was a prisoner
of no beliefs, denied a fair trial,
since I could play either victim or thug,

each working wonders out of his failure
to do the right thing – there's always the wrong.
Child of the Enlightenment, I let off steam
after confirming the air's cold enough,

your loudest disciple, hearing voices,
none yours – the thousands you've heard
weren't either. The proof I'm loyal:
I can't trace where mine come from,

except on rare occasions singers
whose graves we rob return in styles
that whipped both of us into a frenzy
when we were young, and they were lionized,

paid precious metals. Sell their stones.
Hail the virtuosity we'd put behind us.
Hoist their human remains on our shoulders
for this last stage of the decaying process.

THE UNEMPLOYED

Whether your people dropped out of the sky,
or sailed near the wind from distant atolls
when distance meant more than it does now,
is none of my business. I'm unemployed,

but pay your respects, because I fear
nothing so little it becomes less
than it should – can't close a raw deal
seguing soon into the hereafter

you underestimate as vermicular,
or look up to, appear ridiculous.
Don't spare me the superfluous details
I spared you first. I hate imitators,

hammer away until a slight dent
is detectable in the anvil,
and the sun sets in the west, then rises there –
by west I mean, of course, the Far East,

where, in my fantasies, you are dragged,
kicking and screaming. Ronins demand
totem poles your dead ringer was sculpted on
by Abos you could swear you civilized,

their lives, enjoyed to the full by you, over.
Descendants, granted the bar sinister,
bluff that it's best to go out guns blazing.
Best to go out and get some fresh air.

SHOCK AND AWE

We despise your subtropical accent,
although it's roughly the same as ours.
Man isn't rational, boy – boys are.
Coincidentally, eternal youth's

our final offer. You'll owe, in return,
shrugs of the shoulders. Won't teach you manners
I've never quite gotten the hang of,
torn from the womb mature, aging badly,

not raised like you were, or as you,
stating the obvious rarely worthwhile,
a second front opening in the war
I've been waging against a false friend,

a correct one demanding the floor,
convinced, when tanked up, years spent researching
the forgettable weren't a waste – he discovered
peasants in a medieval cathedral

for the first time channelled shock and awe
more fluently than either good or evil.
Unrecorded, their dialogue,
as you wish your speechlessness were.

INNER SANCTUM

Tyranny, memories I'll overthrow.
Luckily, they aren't brick and mortar
holding me to the word I've given,
not to charity, but for free,

my inner sanctum non-habitable,
my favourite sons in the entourage –
fattening them with the calves wasn't hard.
It's too late to find a hungry customer;

they've matured into capable stalkers,
recapture their humanity in public,
genuflect – shameless exhibitionists.
Remains a mystery, if they're watched

by the ghost I will never surrender,
though I may change my mind, the seat
of relatively high intelligence
I can't get to touch down a minute

on the throne. No man rules this world –
if mad, he sacrifices at altars
of divinities nobody else worships
live coals walking on wouldn't purify him.

THE COLLABORATORS

Independence I wouldn't demand, though
where they're respected, I'm for my freedoms,
schedule flights of fancy in a crash course
we teach because it has nothing to teach us,

the anti-occupation demo rousing
a lion sleeping inside me. He roars.
I rat him out. Vets put down this paragon
created unequal before the number

system's invention – I mean its discovery,
your faith misplaced in the infinity
I'd define as completely losing count.
Heaviest boxer here pound for pound,

I could hand-deliver a lecture
on life each calls his; that's our custom.
There's no predicting, as we grow older,
how much less possessive we'll become.

TUNNEL VISION

You're number one, and so am I – reckoning,
in the nautical sense, won't help us
get from point A or B to the ecstasy
with which I cross my legs, and bask,

though it's cloud-capped, brumal at the top,
behaviour here inexplicable,
hence best executed in silence,
a feline you tagged with listening devices

convicted for the ninth life he leads
as if it were his to. Like him, we're hungry,
but is my appetite yours as well?
Each hunts alone, for the nuclear family,

you the person I expected you were.
You shouldn't be; we've hardly met.
Wouldn't know where to start, if the end
weren't visible: a tunnel, my studio's,

where, unrecognizable, you model
for gouaches I hang abroad in the cyclones
we're neither saved nor damned by. They cleanse
palates, skeletons also, and vultures

some estimate have been around the block
a billion times before it was built,
a metropolis demonstrably too small
for the two of us – perhaps more than two.

Each dreams he's primus inter pares,
loves, doesn't need, any introduction,
an insomniac, restless before birth
and after death – the rest isn't composure.

PYRRHIC VICTORY

I was on fire to save you, myself,
and the hoi polloi also if possible,
the house sold out, but narrow aisles
meant the saved were fewer in number

than we might have wished. I lowered the voice
to a lowest common denominator,
finally hollered at my disciples
hanging on words – or were they impaled?

Either way, I had little control
over instincts, least of all mine,
you say you love, and fine then: enjoy,
as you did land we're occupying

till you sign at the bottom motives
you suspect in us are innocent
of any crime except the importance
you give abstractions, and whose fault is that?

I see right through my own curiosity,
get my kicks watching anyone suffer,
could care less if a donkey or bronco
is the support delivering them.

The further from me or closer the end seems,
the more loyalty I swear to mileage,
last stand against incalculability –
feared as much as extinction at my age.

COWBOYS AND BEEKEEPERS

Thanks for the cartoon. Anonymity
rears its, my and your ugly heads.
Come out of hiding and declare
what you threw into the three-ring circus:

illegible land-of-milk-and-honey deeds
cowboys and beekeepers signed over
before they learned to read and write.
Good of you to teach these prisoners of conscience.

Take a trip down – rejoin them. Refresh
their memories, 'holy man of the mountain.'
Should have sold your soul young, just been yourself
on an epic scale more appropriate

when population was low, and elbow room
square kilometres I conquered – because
a chip on my shoulder metastasized?
No, not really – because I felt like it,

my abecedarians whooping instead
of representing the people we aren't,
though they'd be us if they could – too bad
they are the many, we the few.

They have no maps. Ours, I'll redraw.
Isn't itself, their neck of the woods;
needs a rest – something more than a nap,
and less than death, though death wouldn't hurt.

THE PICTURE OF CONCENTRATION

I'm crouching in the landscape's tall grass
you sketched while I studied you closely,
snapping pictures of your concentration
I'm probably incapable of,

supremely bored now, out of my mind,
and plotting a triumphant return
tomorrow. The benefit of the doubt
I won't give you and you can't earn,

the boy next door, his sister too, watched,
standards either records used against you –
encapsulating exactly how,
the aleatory part of my job.

Untimely, those pre-emptive strikes
with which your labourers dug their own graves.
Next time, you hope forces of nature
do the dirty work. Anthropomorphist

syndrome diagnosed, I fake great pity,
then the greatness goes to my head,
teaching me, since your complexion's darker
than it has any human right being,

you'd better behave like an animal –
effectively ending the conversation.
I find, when there's nothing left to prove,
a man becomes perfectly irrational.

THE BARRICADE AUCTION

I'm old enough to surprise my young
fair-weather messmates on the Riviera
when, at last, a harsh winter comes,
a home-field advantage, and I act my age,

forswear unprofessional heroics,
though I'll occasionally fall on my sword.
Antique furniture you donated
proved useful on the barricades

I sold off, the highest bidder
our government whose twisted logic
wasn't vandalized, always looked that way.
Yes, if I recollect correctly,

I was a chair, all but re-elected,
rocking for office. The runners faded,
hadn't trained for marathons I soothsaid
would punish those in the greatest rush.

You couldn't bring their endorphins to heel,
some consolation waiting in wings
you mischievously picked up at school,
taught directions the wind was blowing,

fixed your gaze after gaining altitude,
captivated that much of the planet
answers your thirst for money with water,
integral part of human anatomy.

THE ZODIACAL BEASTS

I'll sign: I misrepresented death,
foamed at its non-existent mouth,
oratory a far cry from knowledge –
the gap in between's my old stomping ground.

There I developed post-domino theory,
a Svengali behind the sages
telling toppled zodiacal beasts,
scrounging for scraps by the moat, to beat it.

Before my birth, I revered newborn elders,
lost a little faith in childhood, the rest
since coming of age. I watched you grow,
then shrink into a constitutional

monarch, mongrel, your master the crown.
I'm loyal to a fault, spit, wipe it clean –
just had it on. Didn't hear the bullet
that can't hear me either; we're equals.

As for the victim, the killer's himself,
not much to go on, our population
mushrooming, increasingly desperate
for solid evidence poverty's shared –

and it is, however imperfectly.
The charities stopped knocking at doors
you, if a foreign aid ship sails in,
will have repaired – till then, they're open.

GREY MATTER

We're good and damaged – our voices can't carry,
bottom of my heart and pit of your stomach
left unbandaged, wounded in action.
You've debriefed a cutting-edge psychologist.

Incurably yourself, you were told health
might mean becoming another person,
hatching. There's neither shell, nor yolk.
Follow the rules: mix yellow and violet

into grey matter. My hypothesis:
life is colourful. We scratch its surfaces,
if I'm right. The day I'm proved wrong,
I'll run away, rejoin the circus,

where round model Earths were my specialty,
flat varieties a tougher juggle.
The crystal ball's in my court now – either it's
buffaloed (impossible), or I am,

poorly positioned near the centre of power
as the regime begins imploding.
For decades, I stuck to my guns, an outsider,
then compromised when nobody was looking.

OUTER SPACE

Given more choice, I'd certainly take it.
Instead, let's conclude I'm indecisive –
better that than the ignoble admission
I'm awaiting orders from above,

immediate superiors polytheists
offing requires divine intervention
tricky under the circumstances;
the gladiators who speak in tongues

are outside my circle I drew freehand.
Insiders lost, ages ago,
a sportsmanship they had, or faked,
when our game was serious. It's still no joke,

and you're winning, relaxed. The nerve –
you beam, inculcated with grace
I deserve. Unjust, my sentence,
commuted from inner to outer space,

trains of thought laid tracks at a loss –
no paying passengers on board,
man of the people, standing ground
I, their absentee landlord, own.

SABOTAGING THE CALENDAR

Often misleading, the mood you're in;
one like a pond takes you out of yourself,
invites a dip difficult to resist
when summering – by the winter solstice,

you are better off anyplace else,
wet and cold, need dry clothes, a change,
and so request an audience the doyen
refuses. Arguably, your half-hour

wait in a blizzard for an answer like that
is predestined, and after the next day
disappears into the subsequent fortnight
you're accused of sabotaging the calendar,

songs you were pencilled in to perform banned
by their composers – ah, to be young again.
But you're living under surveillance,
unlike the powerless chattering classes

who buy your forced cheerfulness at face value,
judge you naive. They're flush, wine and dine
on Halloween while you trick or treat
elsewhere, garbed as a wildcat striker,

blood pressure data news fit to print I,
a trained calligrapher, record shorthand.
Humble words – hear them scraping by
on what they mean, worst kind of peer pressure.

THE MINOTAURS

Fellow Minotaurs laid off at labyrinths
Asiatic Maecenases purchased,
let's contemplate the emerging markets
losing interest in our mythology,

grasp the gravity of the situation,
and the exception that proves the rule:
their reps reached exits before we pounced –
stitch up uniforms; pretend we're doormen,

me spelling out, and you misreading,
my encephalon's contents, wasted.
I insist we lock arms, and agree
on a fast poison for the food-taster

whose job you covet, the belly a joy.
Fire in mine may lustrate, may not –
won't leave ashes bitter in the mouth;
they are all that's left of my taste buds.

HABEAS CORPUS

I've caught traumatic memories experienced
enough to dodge human consciousness
the prime years I was right about everything,
me forgotten now as my predictions

that came true – your media reported
my instincts were down, base, then kicked,
man's warmest contribution his corpse's,
if the last heartbeat comes from the right place.

The dead can't plead ignorance: we record
what happens next even when blows are fatal –
my throat slit during a siesta,
I awoke refreshed in this new world,

captaining ships, pulling strings,
the sailing clear. I'm out of rope,
wasn't numbered among thc prophcts
our special ops left swinging back home.

We issued licences to kill or live,
though the ones you've applied for, to die
under mysterious circumstances,
the late admiral hasn't signed yet,

time passing quickly, slowly as well,
depending on the mood he is in,
sharing it with us a dramatic effort
in which it's every man for himself.

THE MOBS

Anticlimactic, carting martyrs off
after the bloodbath, former butterflies
I immortalized, flattered also,
when painting was king and I court photographer,

a mere mortal – there's no other kind
inducted into your re-education camp.
I'm usually for a little of both,
given a choice between two blunders.

Like your fetuses, I can't behave.
Their excuse: they aren't fully sentient,
with legal rights of the lab's Kalashnikovs,
funny in part-time civilian hands,

rawish recruits consulting lawyers
wise, wise to the ways of the world.
And repetition dulls the senses.
Progress, our kids demand – sadly, the art

of slavish imitation they're against
shares my patron saint, his oath (top secret)
the devil's eye for an eye, two on a bust
well within an iconoclast's reach,

this comrade living in a private hell,
till he offers the red-carpet treatment,
and finds, if he looks too closely,
himself in the middle of the picture

taken, to prove we're all colour-blind,
in the black and white agitprop-meisters
prefer, spectrums uncontrollable
as the mobs. Don't mean those assembled

by the state – ones that form of their own
free will. Mine, I wouldn't share with them,
more like me than they'll ever know –
I ventilate only under my breath.

LEARNING CURVES

Where I'm unwelcome, I directly go.
In the old days, I had too much pride.
Experience taught me: have even more,
a mountain man's as well as a climber's,

and try the patience of a time traveller
whose every stop seems like an eternity.
I was raised awaiting a messiah
I knew inside out till you took me for him,

life here cheap as happiness would be
to a savage in a golden age,
if he had the arithmetic skills
you picked up off a missionary,

swore, oath garbled, recovered, hummed
the unpronounceable. Your hand deserves
a second chance on the holy book –
near-perfect circles, your learning curves.

OVER THE RAINBOW

I am so full of myself when I deal
with others I go through the motions,
and our voices share the speed of sound,
appearances impersonal, yours mine –

don't insist on an explanation,
relations built on the bliss of ignorance.
I'll treat you as a sharp shepherd might
his flock outside a sacred text,

teach an apocryphal lesson or two –
third time lucky in the Church Militant.
I prefer tokens to batons, proof
I'm a tram conductor, not the coup d'état's –

still at large, the maestro responsible,
suddenly dwarfed by monsters he unleashed,
didn't do time hiding in the orchestra
pit into which he simply disappeared.

Hunt the recidivist: savour a stupor
relentless soul-searching throws you into,
perhaps unwilling to believe eyes
I'm for or against shutting completely,

then calm yourself. I'd show you how,
but I've already showered my affections,
and the rainbow I feel coming now
is cold and distant, its colours deceptive.

MARGIN OF ERROR

If you deliver belief in a saviour,
you'll receive my life savings, a sum
almost equal to its margin of error,
price of a holiday in the sun,

where the rich disappear, suffer less
than us voyeurs left behind in limbo,
name we give an introspection
we are constitutionally unfit for,

shuttering windows when tempted to shake
their transparent surfaces for the hell
whose views I'm certain a crash wouldn't change,
plus we'd be left X-raying hands,

vastly preferring the luck of a draw
to either the winners or the losers
sharing our salient character flaws,
why we try to outsmart one another,

help entry-level staff, learn to love
watching ourselves wipe mirrors, such romance
irresistible – we're so repulsive
on the inside we can't look half as bad,

desires burning with no objects in sight.
I advise blaming an arsonist,
and wouldn't bother feigning surprise,
should it emerge you were him all along.

BENEATH THE LEVEL OF CONVERSATION

In the beginning, we were compatriots.
We've become what foreigners should be:
figures of fun I love hating
because they take themselves seriously.

You're glad I lost my public recovering
in a private institution is costly,
yet it's been done, out-of-style incentive
to do anything. Here's how I view things:

not as they are in themselves, or even
as they appear – just under some influence.
We're feted and trashed, a good and bad thief,
but don't exaggerate the difference,

my she-goat, cabbage and wolf stew a hoax,
two out of three ingredients missing –
you're out of your depths, which are my shallows,
so neither one of us learned to swim,

music lovers, conversation beneath us
in the lobby during intermission.
It's less trouble, pretending we're strangers –
bigger, though, letting bygones be bygones.

ACCORDIONIST

The accordion deserves equal billing,
at peace with itself in between shows.
Has nothing on its conscience, the instrument.
If headcases disrupt, the front row's

sub-hypnotist should dial nine-one-one,
new on the job, fired from the old,
despite an Indian summer harvesting
crops whose names the master doesn't own.

And I'm asked why I love the language.
Nobody'd call us pigs at a trough.
We're not there yet – follow directions.
May the Lord grant a second wind, demons

in you because He told them where to go:
this wilderness – for your homecoming,
no scapegoat's either. Irrigation
squads transported the soil you were born on,

not exactly of your own volition,
bird of paradise captured and sold
by fellow natives. Man's at his worst
when he's himself, and now enough

of struggling for half-decent alternatives
generation after generation
ours doesn't outclass, dialogue free
as hydrogen drunk at public fountains.

My acolytes, they love a bargain,
and are agog: yours is a higher
state of consciousness I would let
speak for itself, if it could. It cannot.

A FLIGHT OF STAIRS

I never claimed you were an archangel
invisible to the jet-setting eye
of a designer so busy starving
his runway's lycanthropes they ate him –

their guru: the Rubicon's ferryman.
I pace the bank, weighing pros and cons,
while he contemplates a jump on my scales,
the competition in these parts a travesty –

no decorations should I come in first,
my heart wherever your heart is,
pumping blood, the rest of the body's,
a dirty job we have down to an art,

beneath the radar, under our breaths,
winners and losers at the mercy
of what we can lose, what we can win:
these stairs of yours, for example, a flight,

the protocols of consciousness spoiling
scenery that otherwise wouldn't register.
No diplomat, you cover up
secrets perfectly charming open,

we saints patronizing you incapable
of harder power until we're canonized.
I'll visit heaven even if the trip resurrects
then kills me, the wits battling all mine.

You can't pin life like a wrestler;
it's inside you when you're in the ring.
Let's applaud your loudest detractors –
you chose the wrong sport, crowd noise deafening,

yet retain the right to remain silent
I rarely exercise. It is written:
a man shouldn't fear the sound of his voice
if he's the only fanatic listening.

FALSE FLAG

We're huddled together – stabs in the back
you might interpret as self-inflicted.
I'll campaign in favour of stem cell
research, proving love for the casualties

follows shows of force, almost passes
legislation that routinely dies
on the floor of the house where no grass grows,
because farmers won't vote with gardeners

who neither ignore insults delivered
by their rivals nor stop denying
they could have possibly heard what they heard.
Demand again that they hack the ice,

so we can whip out our rods, go fishing.
Out of spite, they squat meditating –
in our pre-fab monastery no less.
I kick novices seemingly fading,

though in this climate nodding off's a plus.
My clearest views don't interest me
as much as where yours end and another's
begin – can't expedite the transition;

it calls for pampas, a vast buffer zone
through which I'd ride, tall in the saddle
like a gaucho, if the nag weren't a chariot's,
if I weren't preparing a buggy for battle.

ATHELING

Peace, atheling, we freedom fighters
procrastinators who, though we'll become
your allies, aren't yet, seem, in the interim,
unpredictable. You were irrational,

yet still lost the religion. When you stink,
there is no soul to side with against
epiderm you haven't washed for weeks
in solitary, your quondam bookies

my confidential sources – you gambled
on their wrong odds. They apologized.
I wasn't there, but believe me: applause
died at headquarters, where I spank

memoirs out, your finalized draft
of history my first. I'll close your eyes.
I'll bare your fangs, the future tense
an anaesthetic, and I speak its language.

FREEDOM OF ASSEMBLY

Run along into oblivion, or
I will bump you off in the limelight
before your heldentenor imposes
restrictions on the music in my head,

the tunes less globalized than they could be
in various money-spinning ventures
vulgar to the aristocrat in me.
He's equally vulgar – born a peasant,

I celebrated any holidays
we could get, flexibility a sign
from heaven we were on the fast track,
though that interpretation is mine,

mine the glory, and if it turns out
I am wrong, I deserve applause
for essaying the impossible.
Who else around here takes the trouble,

the majority of our population
bowing and scraping as if outnumbered?
I was calculating the ratios
when I received a generous offer

from courtiers hardly worth bringing up,
but we've drifted onto the subject:
I suggest a moment of silence,
more than sufficient – they're alive and well,

each disguised as none of the others.
When he's himself, he improvises,
occasionally speaks his mind, the idiot –
not a mother tongue like you, and I'd

happily leak almost anything
if I were you, as I wouldn't care
about unintended consequences.
I'd only be you temporarily,

the weight of the past unbearable –
a fraction lighter, though, than the present.
By the time it makes me gasp,
I have had a chance to rehearse.

WATERBOARDING

No depths to which my people won't sink;
fortunately, these aren't inside us,
a few underwater, your oilfields
halfway around the globe, most landlocked,

opportunities photojournalists miss
worthless – supply far exceeds demand.
Instruct your lawyer. File for bankruptcy,
while brothers rot in your debtor's prison,

this much learned: fighting to the death
beats either surrender or victory.
You know where you stand, your posture less well,
navel-gazing a discredited option

when the hunger starts. No poaching for
talent unavailable in the food chain
lunch hours at the hourglass factory,
any sand certainly contaminated,

the correct time my least concern,
victim, like you, of uranium poisoning.
You came up with the wildest excuses
for air after the waterboarding,

said one thing, meant another, believed
a third, self-destructive before we arrived
in tall ships. We merely continued
inflicting all you'd inflicted on yourself,

if only, and not only, because
our logic's cold-weather. In wrong climates,
it wilts – a flower, it isn't. A miracle
hatred, though mutual, didn't unite us.

STILL IN THE CAMERA

When the home team bends unwritten rules,
visitors are set free, start scribbling,
what's on my mind just passing through –
the tradition in there isn't hospitality,

the stiff you dropped off today unwelcome.
Only bodies of childhood friends
granted the privilege of growing up
should be brought back down to our level,

surviving heroes advised against
defying a superpower I,
who've served twisting loyally in the wind,
might sabotage from the inside mañana.

Last time I was at the end of my rope,
I envisioned skipping it in heaven.
To perish exploring bang in the doldrums,
you need a single trait: hyperactivity.

I'm the first person I ever controlled –
nostalgia co-exists with temptation
to curse my disputed date of birth,
though I believe in reincarnation,

life after life wish I had control
over either the slaves or the masters.
A neutral observer, I watch revolts,
cheering on the right side, then the other,

help myself, scarcely commit treason,
pick through merchandise, searching for bodies,
admire a few – never mind the reasons.
I'm of the old school, swatting at flies

you keep releasing to irritate me,
and I keep killing. Your endless supply
proves I can't win. We remain close.
Purple prose that justifies your actions

won't do much by way of improving
your bad image, mine still in the camera,
beneath contempt but above suspicion,
unless one dark day the film's developed.

THE NATURALIZATION

Took our telepathized gods seriously
as possible for a while – in the end,
you roared I was all of them, once feared,
rolled into one. Well, monotheist,

look me in the eye, as if it belonged
to forecast hurricane-force winds.
I'm not myself, no more than the cost
of knocking off a luxury item

is its price, and you've paid; you were captured
near your manor, sold into slavery.
I beat you in the humiliation
department, voluntarily relocated

to a continent whose victory over us
I was hired to declare a draw,
each rung of my ladder the last,
and so on ad infinitum – correct me,

for any appearance that's deceptive
is definitely mine. Driven mad,
those whose power overwhelmed us cannot
resist it now – it's all they have left.

If you were dead, you couldn't imagine
dying. Since you can, stop complaining.
I'd plunge in, save your drowning emotions,
if mine were as undisciplined,

and I pushed unflattering comparisons
too far by making them sing like praises –
a citizen of the world's, in theory.
In practice, I'm from where I've been aged.

NOT SO THE OCEAN

Always impolitic, biting the hand
that's the heart and soul of your body.
You would find declaring independence
a hollow victory, and a puppet's.

Go side with light against the visions
I toss and turn expecting, didn't need
when my simoleons could rent first-class
compartments, human beauty sleep

a cause I was unwilling to die for
till I avenged the time to be lost,
my giant footsteps flattening by night
a planet you know perfectly well is round,

though we don't speak merely from experience.
My consolation: neither does thunder,
worshipped, like me, in free-trade zones
demanding my axes, and supplying lumber

on black markets while I sack psittacine
castles in air, in mid-air become
an archaeologist pocketing less than thieves
from whom I buy back my discoveries,

all forgiven. The future is either
in running out of space or insisting
it stand still on your calvary float
for yet another tickertape parade,

a nest resembling a crown of thorns,
and a first drop of water a second.
From my vantage on our bustling shore,
a drop vanishes – not so the ocean.

CLOAK AND DAGGER

Decades of cloak and dagger have changed
our manumitted colony's dress code –
I promised we'd meet the natives halfway,
while making myself completely at home,

etching self-portraits as a fifth column
the viewer's cordially invited to join.
If there weren't persons inside me I'm not,
who'd suffer terror I'm busy enjoying?

Prepare a list. How quickly he's grown,
the ex-blastocyst ensconced in power.
I became somebody ghosting his blow-
by-blow memoir from cover to cover,

throw his weight around, unconcerned
he's looking askance at us; we're aesthetes,
prefer our pure forms to their content served
up as live game, after all, not raw meat,

share with a first tribe a second's illusions
about assorted assets it may claim
for its encampment from the universe,
then wait: they'll squabble over our telescopes.

ACKNOWLEDGEMENTS

Early versions of 'The Good Reason,' 'Contractors,' 'Exact Change,' 'Over the Rainbow' and 'Margin of Error' appeared in *Perihelion*.

'The Picture of Concentration,' 'Atheling,' 'Waterboarding' and 'Not So the Ocean' appeared in *This Magazine*.

I am grateful to the Ontario Arts Council for its support.

I thank my editor, Kevin Connolly, and the book's designer, Alana Wilcox, for their excellent work. Thanks also to Evan Munday, Leigh Nash, Simon Lewsen and everyone at Coach House.

ABOUT THE AUTHOR

Walid Bitar was born in Beirut in 1961 and immigrated to Canada in 1969. His previous poetry collections are *Maps with Moving Parts* (Brick Books, 1988), *2 Guys on Holy Land* (Wesleyan University Press, 1993), *Bastardi Puri* (The Porcupine's Quill, 2005) and *The Empire's Missing Links* (Véhicule Press/Signal Editions, 2008). He lives in Toronto.

Typeset in Freight and Freight Sans.

Printed in February 2012 at the old Coach House on bpNichol Lane in Toronto, Ontario, on Zephyr Antique Laid paper, which was man-ufactured, acid-free, in Saint-Jérôme, Quebec, from second-growth forests. This book was printed with vegetable-based ink on a 1965 Heidelberg KORD offset litho press. Its pages were folded on a Baum-folder, gathered by hand, bound on a Sulby Auto-Minabinda and trimmed on a Polar single-knife cutter.

Edited by Kevin Connolly
Designed by Alana Wilcox

Coach House Books
80 bpNichol Lane
Toronto ON M5s 3J4
Canada

416 979 2217
800 367 6360

mail@chbooks.com
www.chbooks.com